The
TWELVE
DAYS
of
CHRISTMAS

Brian Wildsmith

OXFORD
UNIVERSITY PRESS

The first day of Christmas,
My true love sent to me
A partridge in a pear tree.

The second day of Christmas,
My true love sent to me
TWO TURTLE DOVES, and
A partridge in a pear tree.

The third day of Christmas,
My true love sent to me
THREE FRENCH HENS,
Two turtle doves, and
A partridge in a pear tree.

The fourth day of Christmas,
My true love sent to me
FOUR COLLY BIRDS,
Three French hens,
Two turtle doves, and
A partridge in a pear tree.

The fifth day of Christmas,
My true love sent to me
FIVE GOLD RINGS,
Four colly birds,
Three French hens,
Two turtle doves, and
A partridge in a pear tree.

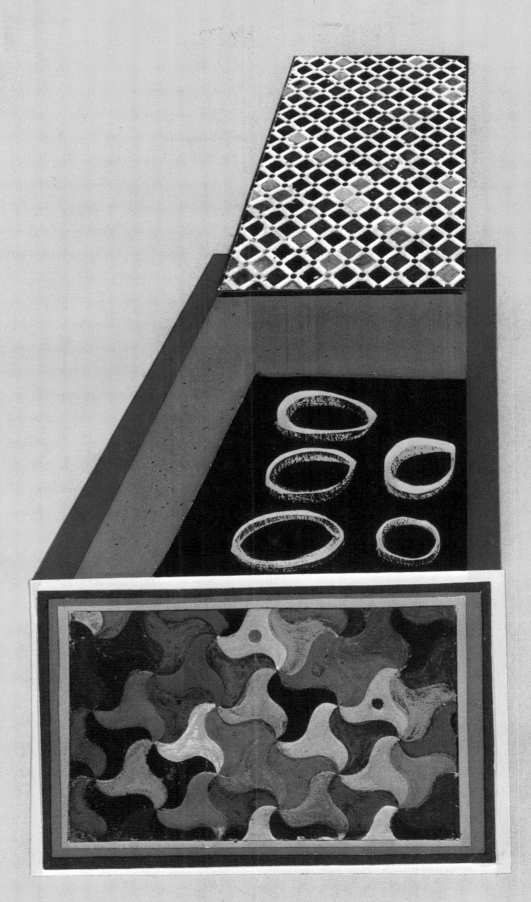

The **sixth day** of Christmas,
My **true love** sent to me
SIX GEESE A-LAYING,
Five gold rings,
Four colly birds,
Three French hens,
Two turtle doves, and
A partridge in a pear tree.

The seventh day of Christmas,
My true love sent to me
SEVEN SWANS A-SWIMMING,
Six geese a-laying,
Five gold rings,
Four colly birds,
Three French hens,
Two turtle doves, and
A partridge in a pear tree.

The eighth day of Christmas,
My true love sent to me
EIGHT MAIDS A-MILKING,
Seven swans a-swimming,
Six geese a-laying,
Five gold rings,
Four colly birds,
Three French hens,
Two turtle doves, and
A partridge in a pear tree.

The ninth day of Christmas,
My true love sent to me
NINE DRUMMERS DRUMMING,
Eight maids a-milking,
Seven swans a-swimming,
Six geese a-laying,
Five gold rings,
Four colly birds,
Three French hens,
Two turtle doves, and
A partridge in a pear tree.

The tenth day of Christmas,
My true love sent to me
TEN PIPERS PIPING,
Nine drummers drumming,
Eight maids a-milking,
Seven swans a-swimming,
Six geese a-laying,
Five gold rings,
Four colly birds,
Three French hens,
Two turtle doves, and
A partridge in a pear tree.

The eleventh day of Christmas,
My true love sent to me
ELEVEN LADIES DANCING,
Ten pipers piping,
Nine drummers drumming,
Eight maids a-milking,
Seven swans a-swimming,
Six geese a-laying,
Five gold rings,
Four colly birds,
Three French hens,
Two turtle doves, and
A partridge in a pear tree.

The twelfth day of Christmas,
My true love sent to me
TWELVE LORDS A-LEAPING,

Eleven ladies dancing,

Ten pipers piping,

Nine drummers drumming,

Eight maids a-milking,

Seven swans a-swimming,

Six geese a-laying,

Five gold rings,

Four colly birds,

Three French hens,

Two turtle doves, and

A partridge in a pear tree.

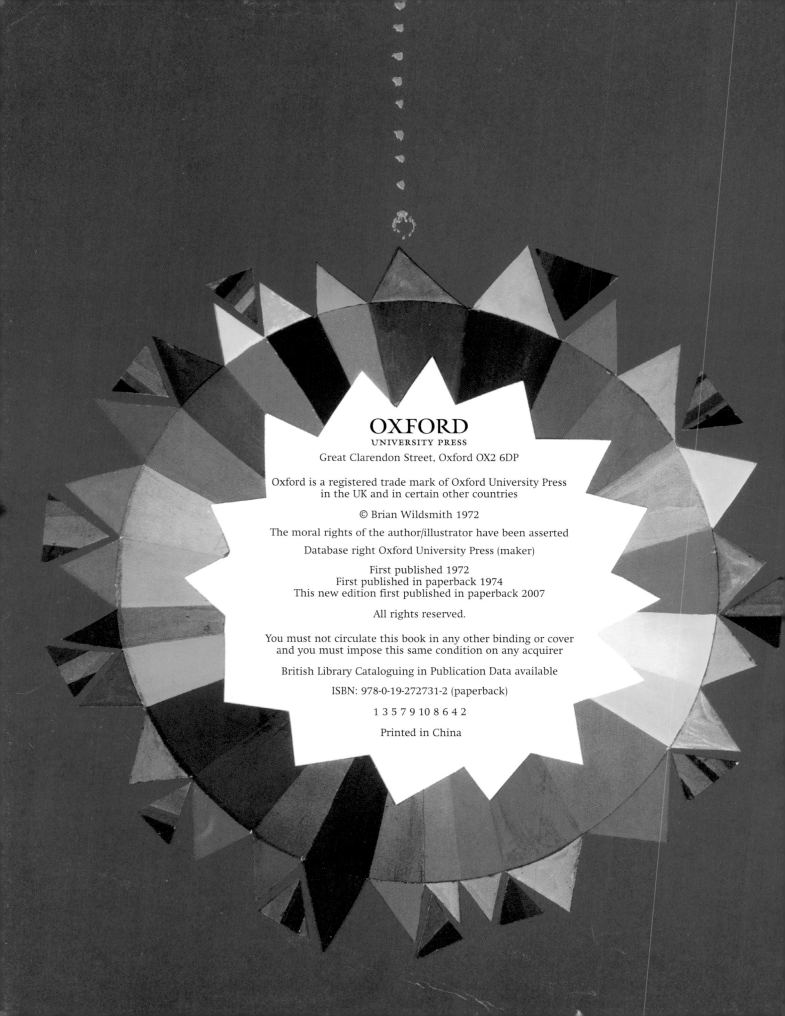

OXFORD
UNIVERSITY PRESS

Great Clarendon Street, Oxford OX2 6DP

Oxford is a registered trade mark of Oxford University Press
in the UK and in certain other countries

© Brian Wildsmith 1972

The moral rights of the author/illustrator have been asserted

Database right Oxford University Press (maker)

First published 1972
First published in paperback 1974
This new edition first published in paperback 2007

British Library Cataloguing in Publication Data available

ISBN: 978-0-19-272731-2 (paperback)

1 3 5 7 9 10 8 6 4 2

Printed in China